Soups
and **More**

ACADEMIA
BARILLA

The Taunton Press

ACADEMIA BARILLA
AMBASSADOR OF ITALIAN GASTRONOMY
THROUGHOUT THE WORLD

Academia Barilla is a global movement toward the protection, development and promotion of authentic regional Italian culture and cuisine.
With the concept of Food as Culture at our core, Academia Barilla offers a 360° view of Italy. Our comprehensive approach includes:

- a state-of-the-art culinary center in Parma, Italy;
- gourmet travel programs and hands-on cooking classes;
- the world's largest Italian gastronomic library and historic menu collection;
- a portfolio of premium artisan food products;
- global culinary certification programs;
- custom corporate services and training;
- team building activities;
- and a vast assortment of Italian cookbooks.

Thank you and we look forward to welcoming you in Italy soon!

CONTENTS

EDITED BY

ACADEMIA BARILLA

PHOTOGRAPHS

ALBERTO ROSSI

RECIPES BY

CHEF MARIO GRAZIA

CHEF LUCA ZANGA

TEXT BY

MARIAGRAZIA VILLA

ACADEMIA BARILLA EDITORIAL COORDINATION

CHATO MORANDI

ILARIA ROSSI

REBECCA PICKRELL

GRAPHIC DESIGN

PAOLA PIACCO

A MILANESE RISOTTO SHOULD NOT BE OVERCOOKED—HEAVEN FORBID! JUST A TAD MORE THAN AL DENTE ON THE PLATE [...]

CARLO EMILIO GADDA,

FROM THE MAGAZINE

IL GATTO SELVATICO, 1959

RICE

Italy's vast cuisine is much like its glorious frescoes—full of vibrant colors and robust elements, as well as more delicate, nuanced touches. In short, apart from Italy's great dishes, those that are famous all over the world, there are also smaller, lesser-known fare that are warm, intimate and redolent of home and family. Rice and soups belong to this category, the "minor" dishes that are decidedly rich in regional specialties and able to reach unparalleled heights.

Academia Barilla, an international center founded to promote Italian cuisine, selected 40 rice and soup recipes from the *Bel Paese* ("the beautiful country," as the Italians call their home). Some, such as baked risotto, were popular among noble families, but most have more humble origins: the best simple and ingenious things are created from necessity, like bread and tomato soup or potato and chestnut soup.

Rice (the genus *Oryza*, a term that probably derives from the ancient state of Orissa in India) is an annual plant of the *Gramineae* family, and, after wheat, the most common grain on earth. There are two cultivated species: the Asian *Ortyza sativa* and the African *Ortyza glaberrima*. From the first, three subspecies have been differentiated: *indica*, from India; *javanica*, widespread in Indonesia; and *japonica*, from which (via hybridization) the Italian varieties are derived. In ancient Rome, rice was a rare and expensive product, imported from the East as a spice and used by women to soften and lighten the skin and by gladiators and athletes as a type of "performance-enhancing substance." Perhaps introduced by the Arabs in Spain in the eighth century, rice then moved to Sicily. The first historical mention of rice being cultivated in Italy (or, more precisely, in Lombardy) is in a letter from 1475, written by Galeazzo Maria Sforza, Duke of Milan. Today, the Italian paddy is the most competitive in Europe for fine-quality rice. Intended mainly for risotto, that cultured and refined ambassador of the "Made in Italy" seal of approval, Italian rice has won over chefs around the world. Easily digested, tasty and invigorating, rice discreetly welcomes any sauce, from the whimsical to the more linear. It lends itself to several dishes: vegetables, wine, cheese, truffles, mushrooms, legumes, fruits, eggs, meat, fish and shellfish. In Lombardy alone, where the first risotto (with saffron) was created in 1574, there are dozens of traditional risotto varieties. It is much the same in Piedmont and Veneto. However, rice dishes are also enjoyed in southern Italy, with the Po Valley proving to be something of a chosen land for the cultivation of rice.

RICE BOMBE

Preparation time: 1 hour   Cooking time: 5 minutes   Difficulty: medium

4 SERVINGS

1 3/4 cups (350 g) **Arborio rice**
2 tbsp. (30 ml) **extra-virgin olive oil**
4 tsp. (20 g) **unsalted butter**, plus
more for the mold
1 small **onion**, finely chopped
7 oz. (200 g) **veal**
1 3/4 oz. (50 g) **calf sweetbreads**, diced
1 3/4 oz. (50 g) **pork sausage**
1 small stalk **celery**, chopped
1 small **carrot**, peeled and chopped
Pinch of **ground cinnamon**

7 oz. (200 g) **canned peeled tomatoes**,
juice drained and seeded
1/3 cup (80 ml) **chicken or beef broth**
Juice of 1 **lemon**
2 large **eggs**
1/3 cup (35 g) grated **Parmigiano-Reggiano cheese**
4 **capers**, chopped
2 oz. (50 g) **breadcrumbs** (about 1/2 cup)
Salt and pepper to taste

Heat the oven to 390°F (200°C). Cook the rice in a pot of boiling, salted water, and when it is half cooked, drain it and set aside to cool.

Meanwhile, in a saucepan, mix together the olive oil and 2 teaspoons of the butter over medium heat and sauté the onion until translucent. Add the veal, sausage and sweetbreads, plus the celery and carrot, and cook until golden. Add the cinnamon, tomatoes, and broth and cook for 40 minutes over low heat. Transfer the rice to a large bowl and add the lemon juice. Add the eggs, the Parmigiano, capers, salt and pepper to taste, and some sauce from the pan and mix well.

Butter a gelatin or timbale mold, sprinkle with some breadcrumbs and spoon in the rice, reserving at least a fifth. Make a deep hollow in the center, spoon in the meat and cover with the remaining rice. Sprinkle with remaining breadcrumbs and small pieces of remaining butter. Bake for about 20 minutes.

RISOTTO
WITH POTATOES AND LEEKS

Preparation time: 10 minutes   Cooking time: 20 minutes   Difficulty: easy

4 SERVINGS

3/4 lb. (320 g) **Arborio rice**
1 lb. (400 g) medium **potatoes**, *peeled and cubed*
1/4 lb. (120 g) **leeks**, *white and light green parts only, sliced*
2 tbsp. (30 g) **unsalted butter**
1 1/2 quarts (1 1/2 l) **vegetable or beef broth**, *heated*
Salt and pepper *to taste*

Melt the butter in a saucepan and sauté the leeks over low heat. Add the potatoes and rice and cook the rice until toasted, stirring to coat with the butter. Add enough broth to cover the rice. Cook, stirring frequently and gradually adding more broth as it becomes absorbed. Continue to cook until all the broth has been absorbed. Season with salt and pepper and serve.

RISOTTO
WITH ASPARAGUS

Preparation time: 15 minutes   Cooking time: 20 minutes   Difficulty: medium

4 SERVINGS

2 1/4 lbs. (1 kg) **asparagus**
1 lb. (500 g) **Arborio rice** *(2 1/2 cups)*
5 oz. (150 g) **Taleggio** *or similar cheese, grated*
1 stick (120 g) **unsalted butter**
1 small **onion,** *chopped*
Salt and pepper *to taste*

Wash the asparagus and cut to equal lengths. Peel the fibrous ends.
Cut the tips off and set aside, then cut the stalks into disks. Boil in a pot of
salted water until cooked but still firm, about 10 minutes. Reserve the asparagus
water (about 6 cups) for cooking the rice.
Sauté the onion in a saucepan with 2 teapoons of butter until translucent. Add
the rice, stirring to coat the rice with butter until rice is toasted. Add the cooking
water from the asparagus, a little at a time, stirring frequently until the rice has
absorbed the water. Add the asparagus (stalks and tips), remaining butter and
the cheese. Season with salt and pepper, stir well and serve.

RISOTTO
WITH PORCINI MUSHROOMS

Preparation time: 20 minutes   Cooking time: 18 minutes   Difficulty: easy

4 SERVINGS

1 1/2 cups (300 g) **Carnaroli rice**
1 small **onion**, *chopped*
6 1/3 cups (1 1/2 l) **beef broth**
1/2 stick (60 g) **unsalted butter**
3/4 cup plus 1 tbsp. (80 g) grated **Parmigiano-Reggiano cheese**
1 tbsp. plus 1 tsp. (20 ml) **extra-virgin olive oil**
11 oz. (300 g) **porcini mushrooms**
1 clove **garlic**
1 tbsp. (4 g) **chopped fresh parsley**
Salt *to taste*

Clean the mushrooms thoroughly, removing the soil and wiping them with a damp cloth. Slice them thinly. Heat the oil in a skillet and brown the garlic. Remove garlic, add the mushrooms (reserving some for garnish) and sauté until browned but still firm. Season with salt and parsley.

Melt 4 teaspoons (20 g) of the butter in a saucepan and sauté the onion. Add the rice and cook until toasted, stirring to coat with the butter. Gradually add the broth, adding more as it gets absorbed. Add the mushrooms and stir to combine. Continue cooking until all the broth has been absorbed, stirring frequently, then remove it from the heat and mix in the remaining butter and Parmigiano. Garnish with reserved mushrooms and serve.

RISOTTO
WITH BARBERA WINE

Preparation time: 10 minutes   Cooking time: 20 minutes   Difficulty: medium

4 SERVINGS

2 cups (360 g) **Baldo or Roma rice**
6 1/3 cups (1 1/2 l) **beef broth**
2 **onions**, *finely sliced*
1 3/4 oz. (50 g) **beef bone marrow**
3 cups (3/4 l) **Barbera wine**
3 tbsp. (50 g) **tomato sauce**
5 tbsp. plus 2 tsp. (80 g) **unsalted butter**
2 3/4 oz. (80 g) grated **Parmigiano-Reggiano cheese**
2 tbsp. (30 ml) **extra-virgin olive oil**
2 fresh **bay leaves**, *plus more for garnish*
1 small **bunch fresh sage**
Pepper and nutmeg *to taste*

Heat the olive oil and 4 teaspoons (20 g) of the butter in a saucepan over medium heat and sauté onions with the beef bone marrow and 2 bay leaves. When the onions are soft, add about 1 1/2 cups wine to the sautéed onions and cook until the wine is reduced. Add the rice, increase the heat and stir with a wooden spoon until the ingredients are thoroughly mixed and the rice is toasted. Dilute remaining 1 1/2 cups wine with a ladle of the broth, then add the wine-broth liquid to the rice mixture. Add the tomato sauce and some sage, reserving some leaves for garnish. Continue to cook, stirring, until the wine is absorbed. Gradually add the broth, adding more as it gets absorbed. Stir in the remaining butter and the cheese, sprinkle generously with pepper and nutmeg. Garnish with bay and sage leaves and serve with a spoon.

RISOTTO
WITH CASTELMAGNO CHEESE

Preparation time: 5 minutes   Cooking time: 18 minutes   Difficulty: easy

4 SERVINGS

1 1/2 cups (300 g) **Carnaroli rice or Arborio rice**
1 small **onion**, *chopped*
1/2 cup (100 ml) **white wine**
6 1/3 cups (1 1/2 l) **beef broth**, *heated*
1/2 stick (60 g) **unsalted butter**
2 3/4 oz. (80 g) **Castelmagno or Gorgonzola cheese**
Salt *to taste*

Melt 4 teaspoons (20 g) of the butter in a saucepan and sauté the onion. Add the rice and cook until toasted, stirring to coat the rice with the butter. Add the white wine and cook, continuing to stir, until the wine is absorbed. Gradually add the broth, adding more as it gets absorbed, while stirring frequently. Remove from heat, season with salt and mix in the remaining butter and the cheese, reserving some cheese for garnish. Scatter the remaining Castelmagno over the risotto and serve.

SQUASH BLOSSOM RISOTTO
WITH CRAB

Preparation time: 10 minutes   Cooking time: 20 minutes   Difficulty: easy

4 SERVINGS

2 cups (320 g) **Arborio rice**
1/2 cup plus 3 tbsp. (165 ml) **extra-virgin olive oil**
8–10 small **crabs**, quartered
5 cups (1 1/4 l) **vegetable or fish broth**, heated
3 1/2 tbsp. (50 ml) **white wine**
1 1/2 oz. (40 g) **pesto**
3 1/2 oz. (100 g) **squash blossoms**

1 1/2 tbsp. (10 g) grated **Pecorino cheese**
2 1/2 tbsp. (15 g) grated **Parmigiano-Reggiano cheese**
2 tsp. (4 g) **pine nuts**
1/4 **garlic** clove
2 tbsp. (4 g) **fresh minced parsley**
Salt and pepper to taste

To make the pesto, blend the squash blossoms (cleaned out and rinsed) with the pine nuts, cheeses, garlic and 1/2 cup of olive oil. Season with salt and pepper. Heat 2 tablespoons of oil in a saucepan. Add the rice and cook until toasted, stirring to coat the rice with the remaining tablespoon of olive oil. Add the white wine gradually, stirring, until the wine evaporates. Add the crabs and continue cooking. Gradually add the broth, adding more as it gets absorbed. Stir in the pesto. Garnish with parsley and serve.

TOMATO RISOTTO

Preparation time: 30 minutes   Cooking time: 18 minutes   Difficulty: easy

4 SERVINGS

1 lb. (500 g) **vine-ripened tomatoes**, *peeled, seeded and diced*
1 tbsp. (15 ml) **extra-virgin olive oil**
1 1/2 cups (300 g) **Vialone nano rice or Arborio rice**
1 small **onion**, *chopped*
1/2 cup (100 ml) **dry white wine**
6 1/3 cups (1 1/2 l) **vegetable broth**, *heated*
1/2 stick (60 g) **unsalted butter**
3/4 cup (80 g) grated **Parmigiano-Reggiano**
Salt *to taste*

Heat 1 teaspoon (5 ml) of the olive oil in a small frying pan and sauté one-third
of the onion until golden. Add half the tomatoes, season with salt and cook for
10 minutes over high heat. Purée the mixture in a blender, then keep warm.
Meanwhile, melt 4 teaspoons (20 g) of the butter in another pan and sauté the
remaining onion until translucent. Add the rice and cook until toasted, stirring to
coat with the butter. Add the wine gradually, stirring continuously, until all the
wine has been absorbed. Add half the puréed tomato mixture and pour in the
broth gradually, stirring, and continue cooking for about 10 more minutes. Add
the remaining tomatoes and season with salt, if necessary. Remove from heat
and fold in the remaining butter and the Parmigiano. Garnish with
the remaining puréed tomato sauce.

TRUFFLE RISOTTO

Preparation time: 10 minutes   *Cooking time: 18 minutes*   *Difficulty: easy*

4 SERVINGS

1 1/2 cups (300 g) **Carnaroli rice or Arborio rice**
1 small **onion**, finely chopped
1/2 cup (100 ml) **white wine**
6 1/3 cups (1 1/2 l) **beef broth**, heated
1/2 stick (60 g) **unsalted butter**
3/4 cup plus 1 tbsp. (80 g) grated **Parmigiano-Reggiano cheese**
White or black truffle to taste, sliced
Salt to taste

Melt 4 teaspoons (20 g) of the butter in a saucepan and sauté the onion until translucent. Add the rice and cook until toasted, stirring to coat with the butter. Add the wine and cook, continuing to stir, until the wine is evaporated. Add the broth gradually, stirring frequently, until the risotto is cooked and the broth is absorbed. Season with salt.

Remove the risotto from the heat and mix in the remaining butter and Parmigiano. Garnish the risotto with the truffles and serve.

MILANESE-STYLE RISOTTO

Preparation time: 30 minutes   Cooking time: 20 minutes   Difficulty: medium

4 SERVINGS

1 1/2 cups (320 g) **Superfino rice or Arborio rice**
2 oz. (50 g) **beef bone marrow**, crumbled
5 1/2 tbsp. (80 g) **unsalted butter**
2 oz. (50 g) **onion**, finely chopped (about 1/3 cup)
1/2 cup (100 ml) **white wine**
4 1/4 cups (1 l) **beef broth**, heated
1 pinch saffron powder (or one .125 g packet) plus 1/4 oz. **saffron pistils**
2/3 cup grated **Parmigiano-Reggiano cheese**
Salt and pepper to taste

Melt half the butter in a saucepan and sauté the onion until translucent. Add the rice and toast for about 1 minute, stirring to coat with the butter. Add the white wine and cook, continuing to stir, until the wine evaporates, about 5 minutes; then add the beef bone marrow. Add the broth gradually, stirring frequently, until the risotto is cooked and the broth is absorbed, about 10 minutes. Add the saffron and season with salt and pepper.

When all the liquid has been absorbed by the rice and it is still al dente, remove from the heat. Whisk in the remaining butter and Parmigiano.

28

RISOTTO
WITH SCAMPI AND ZUCCHINI FLOWERS

Preparation time: 20 minutes   *Cooking time: 20 minutes*   *Difficulty: medium*

4 SERVINGS

1 1/2 cups (320 g) **Arborio rice**
16 **zucchini flowers**
14 oz. (400 g) **langoustine or crayfish**
6 1/3 cups (1 1/2 l) **fish broth**, heated
1/2 **onion**, finely chopped
Extra-virgin olive oil
4 tsp. (20 g) **unsalted butter**
Salt to taste
3 1/2 tbsp. (50 ml) **white wine**

Heat the olive oil in a large saucepan and sauté the onion over low heat for about 2 minutes, until soft and translucent but not browned. Increase the heat to medium, add the rice and toast for about 2 minutes, stirring continuously to coat with the oil. Add the white wine and cook, continuing to stir, until the wine is absorbed. Increase the heat to high and add the broth gradually, stirring frequently so the rice does not stick, until the risotto is cooked and the broth is absorbed. Then add the zucchini flowers and lastly the scampi. When the rice is almost cooked, season with salt and stir in pats of butter. Continue to cook, gradually adding the remaining broth, while stirring frequently.

SOUPS

Is there anything more comforting than a good soup? Few things are better than a steaming hot bowl on harsh winter evenings, or a cool, refreshing soup on hot summer nights. Apart from being a first-class comfort food, soups, more than any other food, provide a dose of home—so much so that the Italian term for soup derives from the verb *minestrare*, a variant of "minister," or "to administer." This is fitting, as it was usually the most influential member of the family who distributed bowls of soup to those gathered around the kitchen hearth.

Vegetable-based recipes have as many variations as there are gifts from the garden. The harvest might include tomatoes, eggplant, pumpkin, broccoli, cabbage, artichokes, chicory and more; and for each there is a soup or stew. Some are light and some are luxurious; some are hearty and some are refreshing; some incorporate pasta or rice—and all taste that much more delicious with a slice of fresh bread beside them. The medieval word *suppa*, in fact, described a slice of soaked bread. At the time, hardened bread often served as plates at the tables of the upper classes. Diners would place pieces of meat and other foods on these bread slices, and once the meal was finished, the bread was cooked in water or broth and then given to servants.

Stews and soups are unlimited in their potential and their ability to adapt and be adapted: The traditional *stracciatella alla romana* (Roman egg drop soup), for example, was until recently only served in Roman restaurants at the start of important meals. Italian soups run the gamut of flavors, encompassing light, rustic vegetable soups, made many different ways from Northern to Southern Italy, to heartier, denser soups made from chickpeas, beans and peas. From fish soups (stamped with regional pride and ingredients from the Adriatic to the Tyrrhenian seas) to chunkier meat stews and broths, the peninsula is a haven for soup lovers of all tastes.

Some of the recipes included in this collection have historical significance, such as the Pavese soup, which was reportedly invented by a Lombardy peasant woman in 1525 to feed King Francis I, ruler of France (and Milan) following his defeat at the Battle of Pavia. Similarly beloved is that of the Valpellinese soup, but its origin is lost in the ancient and humble Aosta Valley gastronomy. Other recipes are new and exquisitely Italian in their inclusion of high-quality ingredients and their mastery of execution and creativity. One only has to look at the barley soup with its vegetables, olive oil, goat cheese and herbs to find a worthy example.

TYROLESE DUMPLINGS

Preparation time: 20 minutes   Cooking time: 15 minutes   Difficulty: easy

4 SERVINGS

1 lb. (400–500 g) **loaf of day-old white bread**
1 1/4 cups (300 ml) **milk**
1 1/3 sticks (150 g) **unsalted butter**, at room temperature
1 1/4 cups (150 g) **all-purpose flour**, sifted
5 large **eggs**
2 tbsp. (8 g) **chopped fresh parsley**
6 1/3 cups (1 1/2 l) **beef broth**, heated
Nutmeg to taste
Salt to taste

Remove the crust from the bread and dice the rest into cubes. Place in a large bowl. Add the following ingredients, stirring rapidly after each addition: first add the butter, then pour the milk in a thin stream. Next add the flour, whole eggs and parsley. Finish by adding salt and a generous sprinkling of nutmeg.

Form the mixture into dumplings the size of eggs and boil them in a pot of salted water for about 15 minutes. Drain the dumplings with a slotted spoon and serve them in soup bowls, partially immersed in broth.

BROCCOLI PURÉE
WITH CROUTONS AND WALNUTS

Preparation time: 20 minutes   Cooking time: 45 minutes   Difficulty: easy

4 SERVINGS

1 lb. (500 g) **broccoli**, *diced, plus more florets for garnish, if desired*
3 medium **potatoes**, *diced*
1 1/2 small **onions**, *sliced*
6 1/3 cups (1 1/2 l) **water**
2 oz. (60 g) **day-old bread**, *diced (about 1 3/4 cups)*
4 **walnuts**
2 tsp. (10 ml) **extra-virgin olive oil**
Salt and pepper *to taste*

Boil the vegetables in a saucepan of 6 1/3 cups salted water.
Purée the boiled vegetables (diluting with water if necessary) in a blender and season with salt and pepper.
Toast the bread on a greased nonstick pan.
Garnish the creamed broccoli with the croutons, a broccoli floret, and the walnuts. Drizzle with olive oil.

FAVA BEAN PURÉE
WITH FRIED CHICORY AND BREADCRUMBS

Preparation time: 10 minutes   Cooking time: 50 minutes   Difficulty: easy

4 SERVINGS

1 1/2 small (100 g) **onions**, *chopped*
1 lb. (500 g) **fava beans**, *blanched and peeled*
1/3 cup plus 1 1/2 tbsp. (100 ml) **extra-virgin olive oil**
1 lb. (500 g) **chicory**
5 oz. (150 g) **day-old bread**, *crumbled (about 3 1/3 cups)*
6 1/3 cups (1 1/2 l) **vegetable broth**, *heated*
Salt *to taste*

Sauté the onions until translucent with one-third of the olive oil in a pot over
medium heat. Add the fava beans and cook for a few minutes, then add the
broth. Season with salt and let the beans cook for 30 more minutes.
Purée the beans in a blender.
Blanch the chicory in salted water and then sauté it in another one-third of the
olive oil. Fry the breadcrumbs in the remaining oil until crispy. Serve the chicory
with the fava bean purée on the side and sprinkle the fried breadcrumbs on top.

EGGPLANT PURÉE
WITH BARLEY AND ZUCCHINI

Preparation time: 30 minutes   Cooking time: 40 minutes   Difficulty: easy

4 SERVINGS

*1 medium **eggplant***
*1 small **potato**, peeled and chopped*
*1 1/2 small **onions**, chopped*
*1 cup (200 g) **pearl barley***
*1/2 medium **zucchini**, diced*
*1 **garlic** clove*
***Fresh sage, thyme and rosemary** to taste*
*6 1/3 cups (1 1/2 l) **vegetable broth**, heated*
***Salt and pepper** to taste*
*2 tbsp. (30 ml) **extra-virgin olive oil***

Peel the eggplant (reserving the skin for garnish) and dice it, then put it in a colander, salt it lightly and allow it to drain for about 30 minutes.
Heat the olive oil in a saucepan and sauté the onion, garlic and herbs. Add the eggplant and let it brown, then add the potatoes.
Season with salt and pepper, pour in 6 cups broth and continue to cook until vegetables are cooked. Purée the contents of the saucepan in a blender. Pour in the barley and let it cook in the vegetable purée, adding more broth, if necessary. Sauté the zucchini and add it to the purée.
Meanwhile, finely slice the eggplant peel, then fry in oil, drain and salt to taste. Garnish the soup with fried and finely sliced eggplant peel, and serve.

POTATO SOUP

Preparation time: 15 minutes   Cooking time: 40 minutes   Difficulty: easy

4–6 SERVINGS

1 1/3 lbs. (600 g) **potatoes**
3 1/2 oz. (100 g) **onions**, *finely sliced*
2 1/2 tbsp. (35 g) **unsalted butter**
6 1/3 cups (1 1/2 l) **vegetable broth or water**, *heated*
4–6 large **croutons**
Salt and pepper *to taste*

Peel and scrub the potatoes. Cut half a potato into thin strips, for garnish, and set aside; cut the remaining potatoes into cubes. Sauté the onion with the butter in a saucepan until translucent. Add the cubed potatoes and brown slightly. Add the broth or water, salt and pepper and cook for about 40 minutes over low heat.
Meanwhile, boil the potato strips in a small pot of salted water.
Blend the potato-broth mixture with a blender or pass the mixture through a vegetable mill. Garnish the soup with the strips of potato and serve with the croutons.

GAZPACHO

Preparation time: 20 minutes   Resting time: 1 hour   Difficulty: easy

4 SERVINGS

6 large **vine-ripened tomatoes**, *peeled, seeded and quartered*
2 small **red onions**, *coarsely chopped*
1/3 large **cucumber**, *peeled in stripes and coarsely chopped*
3 stalks **celery**, *coarsely chopped*
2 large **bell peppers**, *coarsely chopped*
1 clove **garlic**, *finely chopped*
1 sprig **basil**
2 tbsp. (30 ml) **extra-virgin olive oil**
3 cups (150 g) **cubed day-old bread**
Salt and pepper *to taste*

Toast the bread in the oven. Set 1/2 cup chopped onions, cucumbers, celery, and peppers aside for garnish. Sauté the onions, cucumber, celery, bell peppers and garlic with the olive oil in a saucepan until browned. Remove from the heat and add the tomatoes, basil, and bread. Purée the tomato mixture in a blender, season with salt and pepper and refrigerate for at least 1 hour.
Meanwhile, cut the reserved vegetables into small dice.
Serve the gazpacho very cold, garnished with the diced vegetables.

BUTTER GNOCCHETTI

Preparation time: 2 hours 20 minutes   Cooking time: 5–6 minutes   Difficulty: easy

4 SERVINGS

7 tbsp. (100 g) **unsalted butter**
3/4 cup (100 g) **all-purpose flour** *or Italian "00" flour*
3 large eggs
5 cups plus 1 1/2 tbsp. (1 l plus 200 ml) **beef broth**
3/4 cup plus 1 tbsp. (80 g) grated **Grana Padano cheese**

Melt the butter in a saucepan, then stir in the flour.
Stir in 3/4 cup plus 1 1/2 tbsp. broth until a very thick, pureé-like mixture.
Let it cool, then add the Grana Padano and the eggs, one at a time, stirring with
a wooden spoon, to form a dough. Refrigerate the dough for 2 hours.
Using 2 teaspoons or a pastry bag, shape the dough into gnocchetti.
Heat remaining 4 1/4 cups broth in a saucepan over low heat. Drop gnocchetti
into the broth and let cook for about 5 minutes. Ladle the broth and gnocchetti
into bowls and serve.

POTATO GNOCCHI IN BROTH

Preparation time: 1 hour 20 minutes
Cooking time: 2-3 minutes   Difficulty: medium

4 SERVINGS

6 1/3 cups (1 1/2 l) **beef broth**
3/4 lb. (350 g) **potatoes**
2 1/2 tbsp. (35 g) **unsalted butter**
1/2 cup (50 g) grated **Parmigiano-Reggiano cheese**
3 **egg yolks**
Pinch of **nutmeg**
All-purpose flour, *as needed*
Salt *to taste*

Boil the potatoes in a pot of salted water until tender, about 20 minutes;
then peel them.
Transfer to a large bowl and mash them while they're still hot.
Mix in the butter and one-third of the Parmigiano, and season with
a big pinch of salt and nutmeg.
Add the egg yolks and mix to form a smooth dough.
Flour your hands and, using your palms, roll the dough into thin cylinders.
Let the dough sit on a lightly floured surface for about 30 minutes, then slice it
crosswise into small gnocchi.
Bring the broth to a boil in a pot and drop in the gnocchi. As soon they come to
the surface, remove the pot from the heat and serve the soup immediately.
Serve the remaining Parmigiano on the side.

ARTICHOKE AND BACON SOUP

Preparation time: 15 minutes   Cooking time: 35 minutes   Difficulty: easy

4 SERVINGS

4 1/4 cups (1 l) **chicken broth**, heated
6 **artichokes**
3 tbsp. (50 ml) **lemon juice**
4 tbsp. (60 ml) **extra-virgin olive oil**
1 clove **garlic**, crushed
5 oz. (150 g) **bacon**, cubed
2 oz. (60 g) **onion**, chopped
14 oz. (400 g) **pastina** (such as lancette)
2 3/4 oz. (80 g) grated **Parmigiano-Reggiano cheese**
1 tbsp. plus 1 tsp. (20 g) **unsalted butter**

Clean artichokes by slicing at least 1/4 inch (0.5 cm) off the tops and bottoms and removing all the tough outer leaves. Cut the artichokes in half lengthwise and remove the chokes. Cut into thin slices and soak in a bowl of water with the lemon juice to prevent the artichokes from turning black.

Heat 2 tablespoons (30 ml) of the oil in a large skillet and sauté artichoke slices and garlic over medium-high heat for about 5 minutes. Remove from pan and set aside. To the same skillet, add the bacon and fry over medium-high heat until lightly browned. Remove from pan and set aside. Heat the remaining oil in the skillet and sauté the onion for about 2 minutes. Add the pastina and enough broth to cover it; stir and add more broth as needed until pasta is cooked. Add artichokes a few minutes before the end of cooking. When pasta is cooked and the excess broth evaporates, stir in cheese, bacon and butter. Transfer to a serving dish and serve hot.

CHICKPEA SOUP

Preparation time: 10 minutes   Soaking: overnight
Cooking time: 1 1/2 hours   Difficulty: easy

4 SERVINGS

14 oz. (400 g) **dried chickpeas** *(about 2 cups)*
1 1/2 small **onions,** *sliced*
8 1/2 cups (2 l) **vegetable broth**
1/3 cup plus 1 tbsp. (40 g) grated **Parmigiano-Reggiano cheese**
3 1/2 tbsp. (50 ml) **extra-virgin olive oil**
1 **bunch fresh sage**
Salt and pepper *to taste*

Soak the chickpeas in cold water overnight; drain. Transfer them to a pot with
the sage, 3 tablespoons of the olive oil and the onions. Mix well, add the broth
and cook on low heat for 1 1/2 hours. Season with salt. For a creamier
consistency, purée some of the chickpeas and add them back to the soup.
Garnish with Parmigiano, sprinkle with pepper and drizzle with remaining olive
oil.

POTATO SOUP WITH SAFFRON

Preparation time: 30 minutes   Cooking time: 10 minutes   Difficulty: easy

6 SERVINGS

1 1/3 lbs. (600 g) **potatoes**
11 oz. (300 g) **cannarozzetti or spaghetti**, *broken into small pieces*
8 1/2 cups (2 l) **water**
1/2 **onion**, *chopped*
1 **carrot**, *peeled and chopped*
1 stalk **celery**, *chopped*
Saffron threads *to taste*
4 1/4 tbsp. (70 ml) **extra-virgin olive oil**
Salt *to taste*

Sauté the onion, carrot and celery in the olive oil in a large pot over medium heat. Add the saffron, mixing well, and then set aside. Boil the potatoes in a pot of salted water, then peel and dice them. Add the 8 1/2 cups (2 l) water and the potatoes to the pot of saffron mixture; season with salt. Bring to a boil, add the pasta and cook the pasta to desired doneness. Set the soup aside to rest before serving. (This soup can also be made without pasta, but use less water.)

ITALIAN VEGETABLE SOUP

Preparation time: 20 minutes   Soaking: overnight
Cooking time: 1 hour   Difficulty: easy

4 SERVINGS

3 oz. (90 g) **leeks**, *diced*
3 oz. (70 g) **celery**, *diced*
7 oz. (200 g) **potatoes**, *diced*
5 oz. (150 g) **zucchini**, *diced*
3 oz. (80 g) **carrots**, *peeled and diced*
4 oz. (100 g) **pumpkin**, *diced*
4 oz. (100 g) **dried borlotti beans**
(cranberry beans)

4 oz. (100 g) **dried cannellini beans**
4 oz. (100 g) **savoy cabbage**, *diced*
4 oz. (100 g) **green beans**, *diced*
1 **bunch fresh parsley**, *chopped*
1/3 cup (80 ml) **extra-virgin olive oil**
4 1/4 pints (2 l) **water**
Parmigiano-Reggiano, *for garnish*
Salt *to taste*

Soak the borlotti and cannellini beans separately in cold water overnight; drain. Cook the beans in a pot of cold, unsalted water. Bring the water to a boil in a saucepan. Meanwhile, heat half the olive oil in another saucepan and sauté the vegetables for 4–5 minutes over medium heat. Add the boiling water, bring back to a boil, then lower the heat and simmer for 50 minutes. Add the beans and continue to simmer for about 10 more minutes. Season with salt and sprinkle with the parsley. Drizzle each soup bowl with the remaining oil, garnish with Parmigiano and serve.

BARLEY AND LEGUMES
WITH GOAT CHEESE

Preparation time: 30 minutes   Soaking: overnight
Cooking time: 40 minutes   Difficulty: easy

4 SERVINGS

1 1/3 cups (250 g) **barley**
1/2 lb. (240 g) **fresh goat cheese**,
preferably **Caprino**
2/3 cup (60 g) grated **Parmigiano-Reggiano cheese**
10 small **spring onions**, diced
1 small **carrot**, peeled and diced
1/2 small **zucchini**, diced
10 **green beans**, diced
3 small stalks **celery**, diced

1/4 cup plus 1 tbsp. (20 g) **minced fresh chervil**
3 tbsp. (15 g) minced **fresh wild fennel**
1/4 cup plus 2 tbsp. (25 g) **minced fresh parsley**
6–7 **fresh chives**, minced
1/3 cup plus 1 1/2 tbsp. (100 ml) **extra-virgin olive oil**
5 cups (1 1/4 l) **vegetable broth**
Salt and pepper to taste

Soak the barley in cold water overnight; drain. Sauté the vegetables with 2 tablespoons (30 ml) olive oil in a saucepan. Add 2 to 3 tablespoons of the broth and season with salt. Mix the goat cheese with 1 tablespoon olive oil and a pinch of pepper; set aside for garnish.

Boil the barley in unsalted water for 20 minutes. Strain it and rinse it under running water. Continue cooking the barley in a pot, toasting with oil, as you would for risotto, until *al dente*. Add the remaining broth gradually, stirring frequently, until the barley is cooked and the broth is absorbed, about 10 minutes Add the vegetables and season with salt. Stir in the remaining olive oil, herbs and Parmigiano. Top each serving with a dollop of goat cheese, pepper and a drizzle of olive oil.

BREAD AND TOMATO SOUP

Preparation time: 10 minutes   Cooking time: 30 minutes   Difficulty: easy

4 SERVINGS

1 lb. (500 g) **vine-ripened tomatoes**
7 oz. (200 g) **onion**, chopped
1 cup (250 ml) **water**
2/3 oz. (20 g) **fresh basil**, torn
3 cloves **garlic**
1/2 tsp. **chili powder**
1 lb. (400–500 g) **loaf day-old rustic-style bread**, diced
1/3 cup plus 1 1/2 tbsp. (100 ml) **extra-virgin olive oil**
Salt and pepper to taste

Prepare the tomatoes by making an X-shaped incision on the bottom of each tomato and blanching them in boiling water for 10 to 15 seconds. Immediately dip in ice water, then peel them, cut them into 4 sections, remove the seeds and pass the pulp through a vegetable mill.

Heat 1/3 cup olive oil in a saucepan and sauté the onion, garlic (which will later be removed) and chili powder. Pour in the tomato sauce and water and season with salt and pepper. Cover and cook the soup over low heat for 25 to 30 minutes.

Toast the bread in a nongreased nonstick pan. Add the basil and bread to the soup and remove the garlic. Cover the pan and let the bread soften. Drizzle the soup with the remaining oil and serve.

MARCHE-STYLE PASSATELLI

Preparation time: 40 minutes   Cooking time: 3–4 minutes   Difficulty: easy

4 SERVINGS

6 1/3 cups (1 1/2 l) **beef broth**
3/4 cup (100 g) **dried breadcrumbs**, plus 2/3 cup (40 g) **fresh breadcrumbs**
2 large **eggs**
6 1/2 tbsp. (50 g) **all-purpose flour**
3/4 cup plus 1 tbsp. (80 g) grated **Parmigiano-Reggiano cheese**
2 tbsp. (30 g) **unsalted butter** (optional)
Salt and pepper to taste
Nutmeg to taste
Zest of half a **lemon**, grated (optional)

Combine the eggs, breadcrumbs, flour, and Parmigiano, plus butter and zest, if desired, and mix until a soft dough forms. Season with salt, pepper and nutmeg. Wrap dough in plastic and refrigerate for 30 minutes.
Bring the broth to a boil. Press the dough through a potato masher with large holes, a ricer or a passatelli iron, cutting the dough in 1 to 1 1/2-inch (3-4 cm) noodles over the soup. Continue until all the dough has been used.
Simmer the passatelli over low heat until all the noodles surface, 3–4 minutes. Ladle the soup into bowls and serve.

PASTA WITH CHICKPEAS

Preparation time: 30 minutes   Soaking: overnight
Cooking time: 2 hours   Difficulty: medium

4 SERVINGS

5 (150 g) **cannolicchi pasta** (or other short grooved tube pasta)
5 cups (1.2 l) **water**
10 1/2 oz. (300 g) **dried chickpeas**
1 clove **garlic**, chopped
2 **salted anchovies**, chopped
1/4 cup (60 ml) **extra-virgin olive oil**
Sprigs of fresh **rosemary**
1 oz. (30 g) **tomato paste**
Salt and pepper to taste

Soak the chickpeas in cold water overnight; drain. Boil the chickpeas in a pot of salted water with the rosemary for 1 1/2 hours.
Meanwhile, in another saucepan, heat 1/4 cup olive oil and sauté the garlic and anchovies. Dilute the tomato paste in a bit of the cooking water from the chickpeas, add to anchovy mixture and cook for 10 minutes. Remove rosemary from pot of chickpeas and add chickpeas and cooking water to anchovy mixture. Bring to a boil, add the pasta, season with pepper and cook pasta to desired doneness. (The soup should be quite thick.)

DITALINI AND BEANS

Preparation time: 20 minutes   Soaking: overnight
Cooking time: 1 hour   Difficulty: easy

4 SERVINGS

7 oz. (200 g) **dried white beans**
7 oz. (200 g) **dried cannellini beans**
7 oz. (200 g) **dried borlotti beans** *(cranberry beans)*
2 tbsp. (30 ml) **extra-virgin olive oil**
7 oz. (200 g) **onion**, *chopped*
4 oz. (100 g) **carrots**, *peeled and chopped*
4 oz. (100 g) **celery**, *chopped*
1 **sprig fresh thyme**
5 oz. (150 g) **ditalini** *(or other small pasta)*
8 1/2 cups (2 l) **water**
Salt and pepper *to taste*

Soak all the beans separately in cold water overnight; drain. Heat the oil in a
saucepan and sauté the vegetables. Add the beans and the thyme leaves, cover
with cold water and cook, about 40 minutes. Season with salt and pepper, add
the ditalini and continue to cook, about 10 minutes.

PASTINA IN FISH BROTH

Preparation time: 40 minutes   *Cooking time: 30 minutes*   *Difficulty: high*

4 SERVINGS

7 oz. (200 g) **octopus**
14 oz. (400 g) **tub gurnard or cod**
1/4 lb. (120 g) **mullet**, or any white-fleshed
fish such as haddock, sole or flounder
2 oz. (50 g) **squid**, sliced into rings
7 oz. (200 g) **small cuttlefish**
4 oz. (100 g) **mussels**
4 oz. (100 g) **clams**
1/3 cup plus 1 1/2 tbsp. (100 ml) **extra-
virgin olive oil**

7 oz. (200 g) **pastina**, such as ditalini
2 cups (500 ml) **water**
1/3 cup finely chopped (50 g) **onion**
4 **plum tomatoes**, or 3/4 lb. (350 g)
whole tomatoes
1 tbsp. (4 g) **minced fresh parsley**
Salt and black pepper (or hot red
pepper flakes) to taste
8 slices **rustic bread** (optional)

Rinse the clams, flushing out any sand. Thoroughly scrape the mussels and clean and remove the beards. Clean the fish fillets and cut them into 3/4 to 1 inch (2-3 cm) diamonds. Clean the cuttlefish and octopus, and rinse the squid. Sauté the onion in the oil in a covered saucepan. Meanwhile, peel the tomatoes, remove the seeds, and slice them very thinly. When the onion has turned golden brown, add the tomatoes and cook for 5 minutes, then add all the fish. Season with salt and cook for 15 to 20 minutes, adding a few ladlefuls of hot water as needed. Separately boil the pastina in salted water and strain when it's halfway done. When the fish is ready, add the pastina and let it finish cooking in the fish broth. Serve it very hot with parsley, ground black pepper (or hot red pepper flakes) and slices of toasted rustic bread, if desired.

EGG PASTA WITH PEAS

Preparation time: 30 minutes   Cooking time: 30 minutes   Difficulty: medium

4 SERVINGS

10 1/2 oz. (300 g) **flour** *(about 2 1/2 cups)*
3 large **eggs**
3 1/2 tbsp. (50 ml) **white wine**
1 **onion**, *finely chopped*
1 3/4 lb. (800 g) **fresh peas**
7 oz. (200 g) **bacon**
5 cups (1.2 l) **water**
2 tbsp. (30 ml) **extra-virgin olive oil**
Salt *to taste*

Mix the flour and eggs until a smooth dough forms. Cover and let the dough rest for about 20 minutes. Roll the dough out into thin pasta sheets, cut it into 1/3-inch (1 cm) wide strips and then cut into squares ("quadrucci").
Let dry on a well-floured tray.
Sauté the onion in the olive oil over medium heat. Add the bacon and gently fry until crisp, add the white wine and cook until it evaporates completely. Add the peas and cover with the 5 cups water. Simmer for about 20 minutes and then add the quadrucci pasta. Season with salt and continue cooking over medium heat until the pasta is al dente, or to desired doneness. Serve the quadrucci with some of the cooking liquid.

SPAGHETTI WITH BROCCOLI

Preparation time: 40 minutes   Cooking time: 6 minutes   Difficulty: medium

4 SERVINGS

12 oz. (350 g) **spaghetti**, *broken in half*
1 lb. (500 g) **broccoli**
2 oz. (60 g) **prosciutto** *(dry-cured), sliced*
2 oz. (60 g) **pork rinds**
1 tbsp. plus 1 tsp. (20 ml) **extra-virgin olive oil**
1 1/2 small **onions**, *sliced*
1 clove **garlic**, *crushed*
1/2 cup plus 1 1/2 tbsp. (60 g) grated **Pecorino Romano cheese**
4 1/4 cups (1 l) **water**
Salt and pepper *to taste*

Divide the broccoli into florets, wash thoroughly, and boil it in lightly salted water on medium heat until cooked. Remove from heat and set aside.

Sauté the onions and garlic in the olive oil until golden brown, then add the prosciutto. Mix well and add the water.

Meanwhile, clean the pork rinds very carefully, removing any hairs and slicing the pork thinly. Blanch the pork in unsalted water, then add to the pot with the prosciutto and 4 1/4 cups water. Bring the pot to a boil, add a pinch of salt and pepper and let it cook for about 5 minutes. Add the spaghetti and cook to desired doneness in the soup. Add the broccoli florets with some of the broccoli water (the soup should be slightly dense) and continue to cook for a few more minutes. Garnish with Pecorino and a generous sprinkling of pepper.

ROMAN EGG DROP SOUP

Preparation time: 10 minutes   Cooking time: 1–2 minutes   Difficulty: easy

4 SERVINGS

4 large **eggs**
4 1/4 cups (1 l) **chicken broth**
1/2 cup (50 g) grated **Parmigiano-Reggiano cheese**
Salt *to taste*

Whisk the eggs in a bowl with the Parmigiano.
Bring the broth to a boil and add the egg-and-Parmigiano mixture. Cook for
about 2 minutes, whisking constantly. Season with salt before serving.

POTATO AND PUMPKIN SOUP

Preparation time: 20 minutes   Soaking: overnight
Cooking time: 45 minutes   Difficulty: easy

4 SERVINGS

1 lb. (500 g) **pumpkin**, *peeled and chopped*
3 medium **potatoes**, *peeled and chopped*
1 1/2 small **onions**, *sliced*
1 cup (200 g) **cannellini beans**
6 1/3 cups (3 1/2 l) plus 8 1/2 cups (2 l) **water**
1 **sprig thyme**, *minced*
1 **sprig rosemary**, *minced*
2 tsp. (10 ml) **extra-virgin olive oil**
Salt and pepper *to taste*

Soak the dried beans in cold water overnight; drain. Place the pumpkin, potatoes, onions and 6 1/3 cups (3 1/2 l) water in a saucepan and bring to a boil. Simmer until vegetables are cooked, then purée in a blender with the liquid they cooked in. Dilute with a bit of water, if necessary, and season with salt and pepper.

Separately boil the beans in about 8 1/2 cups (2 l) water. Stir the beans into the potato and pumpkin soup. Garnish each serving with thyme and rosemary, pepper and a dash of olive oil.

LEGUME AND WHOLE GRAIN SOUP

Preparation time: 20 minutes   Soaking: overnight
Cooking time: 1 hour   Difficulty: easy

4 SERVINGS

*1/2 cup **pearl barley***
*5 cups (1.2 l) **water***
*1/2 cup **spelt***
*1/2 cup **dried lentils***
*1/2 cup **dried borlotti beans** (cranberry beans)*
*3/4 cup **frozen peas***
*1 small **potato***
*1 tbsp. plus 2 tsp. (25 ml) **extra-virgin olive oil***
*Half clove **garlic***
***Fresh thyme** to taste*
***Salt and pepper** to taste*

Soak the dried legumes and grains separately in cold water overnight; drain. Strain the legumes and put them in a large pot with the potato, garlic and thyme. Add the water and bring to a boil. Add the grains and cook according to times on package instructions. Toward the end of cooking, season the soup with salt, add the peas and cook for about 3 more minutes. Garnish the soup with pepper and a drizzle of olive oil and serve.

POTATO AND CHESTNUT SOUP

Preparation time: 20 minutes   Soaking: overnight
Cooking time: 1 hour 20 minutes   Difficulty: easy

4-6 SERVINGS

*7 oz. (200 g) **dried chestnuts***
*1/2 lb. (250 g) **potatoes**, peeled and cubed*
*2 oz. (50 g) **leeks** (whites only), finely chopped*
*4 oz. (100 g) **onions**, finely chopped*
*2 1/2 tbsp. (35 g) **unsalted butter***
*4 1/4 cups (1 l) **vegetable broth***
*2 cups (500 ml) **milk***
*4–6 large **croutons***
*1 tbsp. plus 1 tsp. (20 ml) **extra-virgin olive oil***
***Salt and pepper** to taste*

Soak the dried chestnuts in cold water overnight; drain.
Melt the butter in a skillet and sauté the leeks and onions until browned.
Add the potatoes and chestnuts and sauté briefly. Add the broth and milk,
season with salt and pepper and cook for about 1 hour and 15 minutes
over low heat.
Purée in a blender, or if you prefer more rustic, leave soup as is.
Serve, accompanied by the croutons and a drizzle of olive oil.

FISH STEW

Preparation time: 40 minutes   Cooking time: 50 minutes   Difficulty: easy

4 SERVINGS

2 1/4 lbs. (1 kg) **fish** (such as prawns, mussels, squid, and haddock or cod)
6 1/3 pints (3 l) **water**
2 cups (500 ml) **white wine**
1/2 **lemon**
1 stalk **celery**
2 **onions** (1 chopped)
1 **carrot**, peeled

1 **tomato**
3 1/2 tbsp. (50 g) **unsalted butter**
3 1/2 tbsp. (50 ml) **olive oil**
1 clove **garlic**, chopped
3 tbsp. (15 g) **chopped fresh parsley**
1 3/4 oz. (50 g) **tomato sauce**
Salt and pepper to taste

Clean and wash the seafood, then place the seafood and the 6 1/3 pints (3 l) water, white wine, lemon, celery, carrot, tomato and whole onion in a large pot. Bring to a boil, then lower heat and continue to simmer until the seafood is cooked through. Drain and fillet the fish, reserving the fish broth.

Heat the butter and olive oil in a large skillet, and sauté the chopped onion and garlic over medium heat for about 2 minutes. Add the fish and simmer for 2 minutes. Add the tomato sauce and cook for another 10 minutes.

Season with salt and pepper.

Strain the fish broth and add enough to the skillet to create a thick soup, then continue to cook for another 10 minutes. Garnish with parsley and serve.

TOMATO SOUP

Preparation time: 10 minutes   Cooking time: 30 minutes   Difficulty: easy

4 SERVINGS

2 1/4 lb. (1 kg) **vine-ripened tomatoes**
1 1/2 small **onions**, *chopped*
1 cup (20 g) **chopped fresh basil**, *plus sprigs for garnish*
1 clove **garlic**
7 oz. (200 g) **day-old Tuscan-style bread**, *sliced*
1/3 cup plus 1 1/2 tbsp. (100 ml) **extra-virgin olive oil**
Salt and pepper *to taste*

Prepare the tomatoes by making an X-shaped incision on the bottom of each tomato and blanching them in boiling water for 10 to 15 seconds. Immediately dip the tomatoes in ice water, then peel them, cut them into four sections, remove the seeds and pass the pulp through a vegetable mill.
Heat 1/3 cup olive oil in a pan and sauté the onions and garlic (which will later be removed). Add the tomato purée, cover and simmer on low heat for 25 to 30 minutes. Season with salt and pepper, add the basil and remove the garlic. Toast the bread on a nongreased nonstick pan. Drizzle with remaining oil and serve with the crostini.

PUMPKIN SOUP

Preparation time: 20 minutes   Cooking time: 2 hours   Difficulty: easy

6 SERVINGS

4 lb. (1.8 kg) **pumpkin**
2/3 cup (60 g) grated **Parmigiano-Reggiano cheese**
2 tbsp. (8 g) **chopped fresh parsley**
4 leaves fresh **basil**
1 stalk **celery**
2 sprigs **thyme**
1 clove **garlic**
3 cups (3/4 l) **vegetable broth**, heated; plus more if needed
2 tbsp. (30 g) **unsalted butter**
Salt and pepper to taste

Heat the oven to 450°F (230°C). Create a soup tureen with a lid: Cut off the top cap of the pumpkin and remove all the seeds and filaments.

Sauté the parsley, basil, celery and thyme in the butter for 2 to 3 minutes. Add the sautéed mixture, plus the broth, garlic, cheese, salt and pepper into the pumpkin, stir well and place the lid on the pumpkin.

Bake for about 2 hours. Transfer the pumpkin to a serving plate, take off the lid, remove the garlic, and, with a serving spoon, scrape down the pumpkin flesh and mix it slowly into the broth to make the soup. (Take care to leave enough flesh to support the walls of the "tureen.") If the soup is too thick, add some more hot broth, if necessary. Serve hot.

PAVIA-STYLE SOUP

Preparation time: 20 minutes   Difficulty: easy

4 SERVINGS

2 tbsp. (30 g) **unsalted butter**
8 slices **day-old bread**
4 large **eggs**
4 1/4 cups (1 l) **beef broth**
Generous 3/8 cup (40 g) grated **Grana Padano cheese**
Salt *to taste*

In a pan, fry the bread in butter until golden. Meanwhile, bring the broth to a boil. Then put the bread slices on the bottom of 4 heatproof bowls. Break an egg into each bowl, sprinkle Grana Padano on top and season with salt. Pour the broth over the cheese, being careful not to break the egg, and serve immediately.

Note: Although the boiling broth partially cooks the eggs in the bowl, you may wish to poach the eggs thoroughly in the broth before placing in bowl, to avoid any chance of foodborne illness from raw eggs.

VALPELLINE SOUP

Preparation time: 30 minutes   Cooking time: 30 minutes   Difficulty: easy

4 SERVINGS

1 lb. (400–500 g) **day-old rustic-style bread**, *sliced*
1 lb. (500 g) **savoy cabbage**, *sliced*
6 1/3 cups (1 1/2 l) **beef or vegetable broth**
7 oz. (200 g) **Fontina cheese**, *sliced*
3 1/2 tbsp. (50 g) **unsalted butter**

Heat the oven to 350°F (180°C). Toast the bread with the butter in a skillet
or in the oven.
Meanwhile, bring the broth to a boil in a pot and blanch the cabbage leaves,
then drain. Arrange a layer of cabbage leaves in a baking dish. Top with a layer
of the bread, with the slices overlapping, and cover with the slices of Fontina.
Continue until you have used all the ingredients, finishing with the cheese.
Cover everything with boiling broth and bake for about 30 minutes.

INGREDIENTS INDEX

PHOTO CREDITS

All photographs are by ACADEMIA BARILLA except the following:
pages 6, 95 ©123RF

· · · · · · · · · · · · ·

The Taunton Press
Inspiration for hands-on living®

The Taunton Press, Inc.
63 South Main Street
PO Box 5506, Newtown, CT 06470-5506
e-mail: tp@taunton.com

Translations:
Catherine Howard - Mary Doyle - John Venerella - Free z'be, Paris
Salvatore Ciolfi - Rosetta Translations SARL - Rosetta Translations SARL

LIBRARY OF CONGRESS CATALOGING-IN-PUBLICATION DATA IN PROGRESS
ISBN: 978-1-62710-046-5

Printed in China
10 9 8 7 6 5 4 3 2 1